Who eats who in the Rain Forest?

Robert Snedden

A+
Smart Apple Media

First published in 2005 by Franklin Watts
96 Leonard Street, London EC2A 4XD

Franklin Watts Australia
45–51 Huntley Street, Alexandria NSW 2015

Designer: Cali Roberts, Editor: Sarah Ridley, Art Director: Peter Scoulding,
Editor-in-Chief: John C. Miles, Picture Research: Diana Morris, Artwork: Ian Thompson

PICTURE CREDITS
Andrew Brown/Ecoscene: 18tr. John Cancalosi/Still Pictures: 5, 22. Stephen Coyne/
Ecoscene: 4. Ecoscene: 18bl. Romain Garrouste/Still Pictures: 10. Michael Gore/
Ecoscene: 17. Simon Grove/Ecoscene: 13. Martin Harvey/Still Pictures: 8, 20, 24. Adrian
Hepworth/NHPA: 23. David Hosking/FLPA: 27. Wayne Lawler/Ecoscene: 12. Luiz C. Marego/Still
Pictures: 15b, 16, 25. Robert Pickett/Ecoscene: 19b, 26. Knell Sandved/
Ecoscene: 14. Dr. Patricia Schulz/Still Pictures: 7. Hans Thomashoff/Still Pictures: front
cover, 1. S. Tiwari/Ecoscene: 9,15t. Heinrich Van Den Berg/WWI/Still Pictures: 11. Alan
Watson/WWI/Still Pictures: 21. David Woodfall/Still Pictures: 6.

Published in the United States by Smart Apple Media
2140 Howard Drive West, North Mankato, Minnesota 56003

Library of Congress Cataloging-in-Publication Data

Snedden, Robert.
Who eats who in the rain forest? / by Robert Snedden.
p. cm. — (Food chains in action)
Originally published: London : Franklin Watts, 2005.
Includes bibliographical references.
ISBN-13 : 978-1-58340-961-9
1. Rain forest ecology—Juvenile literature. 2. Food chains (Ecology)—Juvenile literature.
I. Title. II. Series.

QH541.5.R27S64 2005
577.34'16—dc22   2005052056

9 8 7 6 5 4 3 2 1

Note to parents and teachers
Every effort has been made to ensure that the Web sites in this book are suitable for children, that they
are of the highest educational value, and that they contain no inappropriate or offensive material.
However, because of the nature of the Internet, it is impossible to guarantee that the contents of these
sites will not be altered. We strongly advise that Internet access be supervised by a responsible adult.

Contents

Food and energy

All organisms (living things) share certain basic needs. One of these is the need for a place to live where an organism can find everything necessary for survival. This place is known as a habitat.

Every living thing is adapted to life in its habitat. A whale's habitat can be as vast as the ocean, whereas a tadpole's habitat can be as tiny as a pool of water trapped in a flower.

Energy is essential

All organisms need energy to live; they get this from their food. Plants make their own food through a process called photosynthesis. They capture energy from sunlight and use it to make sugar from simple chemicals. This provides the plant with energy, fueling new growth.

Photosynthesis factory: a tropical rain forest in Sri Lanka.

A chain begins

Unlike plants, animals cannot make their own food. They have to find it within their habitat. Many animals eat plants. By doing so, they ingest (take in) a share of the energy that the plants captured from the sun. Other animals eat these plant-eaters, and energy is passed along from one living thing to another. This forms a food chain, like the example on the right, joining plants and animals together.

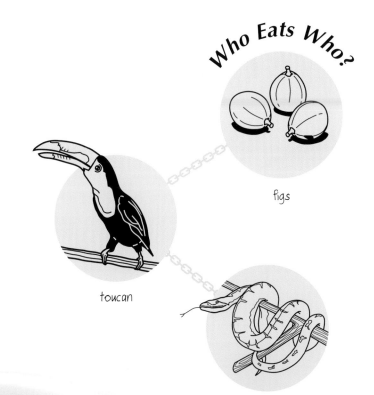

figs

toucan

emerald boa

Ancient forests

Rain forests are the oldest forests in the world. Over thousands of years, the plants and animals living there have developed different ways of feeding and avoiding being eaten. In the process, many food chain links have been forged between forest organisms.

The toucan uses its huge beak to pluck fruit and small animals from rain forest trees.

First link

Plants are at the beginning of almost every food chain. Tropical rain forests provide the perfect habitat for plant growth, as conditions in a rain forest are warm and wet all of the time. Rain forest trees shed old leaves and produce new ones year-round.

Primary producers

Trees and plants growing in a rain forest are known as primary producers because they make, or produce, their own food through photosynthesis. They capture energy from sunlight and store it in their leaves, stalks, and roots. This energy is available to all of the other living things, such as sloths and jaguars, higher up the rain forest food chains.

Who Eats Who?

jaguar

This area of rain forest is part of Canaima National Park in Venezuela.

sloth

leaves

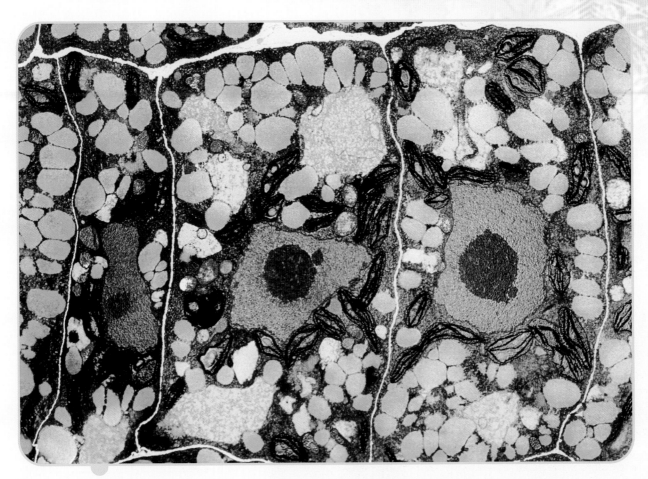

Magnified plant cells. Plants make their own food from sunlight, carbon dioxide, and water.

How photosynthesis works

Plants use the energy of sunlight to join carbon dioxide from the air with water from the soil. Using these two ingredients, the plant makes glucose, a type of sugar. Along with minerals drawn from the soil, plants use this sugar to make new plant material.

Scientists estimate that every year, in every square yard (0.8 sq m) of rain forest, plants produce more than four pounds (1.8 kg) of new plant material. That's a lot of food!

Producer and consumer

Some rain forest plants show up farther along the food chain. The pitcher plant of Southeast Asia grows up to 33 feet (10 m) tall and has pitcher-shaped leaves. These contain a nectar that insects love to drink.

Insects drop in for a nectar snack but quickly find out they cannot escape up the slippery insides. The plant digests and gains nutrients from the insects, much like taking a vitamin supplement!

Linking together

The next links in a food chain are the animals. They cannot make their own food and have to eat the food that is produced by plants or by other animals that have eaten plants. For this reason, animals are called consumers.

This African mountain gorilla is a primary consumer.

Primary consumers

The first animals in the chain are the plant-eaters (or herbivores). They are known as primary consumers. The primary consumers of the rain forest range from tiny leaf-boring insects to big mountain gorillas. However, most primary consumers are insects.

An incredible number of insects live in rain forests. Scientists who study rain forests believe there may be as many as 30 million different kinds of insects living there.

Living larder

Only a very dim light reaches the rain forest floor, so plants grow poorly at ground level. This means there is not much to eat on the forest floor. For this reason, many large primary consumers live high up in the trees. The trees aren't just home for these animals; they are also where the animals find their food supply.

Secondary consumers

Plant-eaters always have to be on the alert for other animals that might want to eat them. Animals that eat other animals are known as secondary consumers, or carnivores. In the rain forest, these include insects, spiders, giant centipedes, reptiles, birds, and big cats.

Changing places

Animals don't always occupy the same place in the food chain. For example, a bird might eat an insect that had been nibbling a leaf, or it might eat a spider that had eaten an insect. So the bird can be both a secondary consumer and a tertiary consumer.

We're in the chain!

More than 3,000 different types of fruits grow in the rain forest. Forest people eat about 2,000 of them.

Secondary consumer: a praying mantis eats a moth on a flower head.

Weaving the web

A food chain is a simple way of showing how one living thing eats another, but it only tells part of the story. Rarely is one type of plant eaten by only one type of animal.

Adapt to survive

Usually animals eat—and are eaten by—different things, so they are part of more than one food chain. An animal with a wide diet has a better chance of surviving, because if one type of food source becomes scarce, the animal can eat something else.

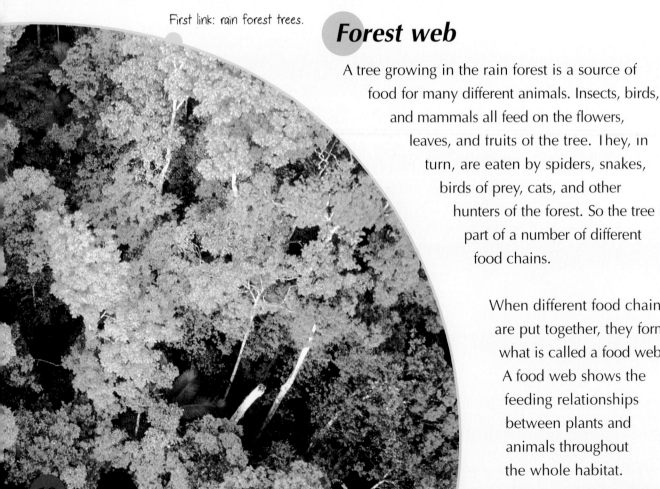

First link: rain forest trees.

Forest web

A tree growing in the rain forest is a source of food for many different animals. Insects, birds, and mammals all feed on the flowers, leaves, and fruits of the tree. They, in turn, are eaten by spiders, snakes, birds of prey, cats, and other hunters of the forest. So the tree is part of a number of different food chains.

When different food chains are put together, they form what is called a food web. A food web shows the feeding relationships between plants and animals throughout the whole habitat.

Climbing the pyramid

How many animals are there at each link of the chains that make up the food web? If you draw this number as a diagram, you get a food pyramid. Many plants support the plant-eaters and meat-eaters above them. This is a useful way to think about how food chains and webs work.

As you can see, it takes a lot of plants to provide enough energy to feed only a few plant-eaters. The plant-eaters then support an even smaller number of meat-eaters.

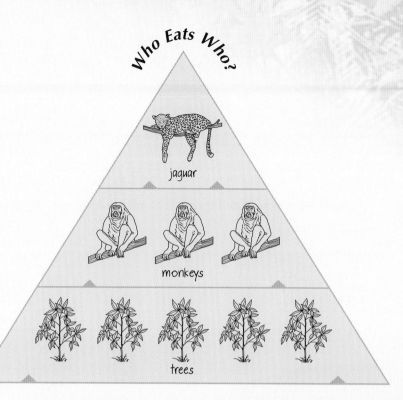

Who Eats Who?

jaguar

monkeys

trees

Losing energy

At every link, a little energy is lost. Plants don't store all of the energy they capture from the sun. They need to use some of it to stay alive and to continue growing.

Plant-eaters almost never eat and digest whole plants, and meat-eaters almost never eat and digest whole plant-eaters. This means that some energy is lost at every link in the chain.

Top of the pyramid: a South American jaguar.

Waste not, want not

Rain forests contain a greater abundance of life, and in greater numbers, than any other habitat in the world. You might think this is because rain forests grow on very fertile soils.

Nutrient loss

Rain forests actually grow on very poor soil. The high temperatures and heavy rainfall of the rain forest climate remove the nutrients from the soil much more quickly than in colder climates. So, what is the secret of rain forest growth?

Rain forest recycling

Leaves, animal droppings, and other materials fall to the forest floor from the trees above. These are swiftly eaten by ants and other small animals. This is the first step in the rain forest recycling process.

Next, bacteria—microscopic organisms that thrive in the warmth of the rain forest—along with fungi that grow among the tree roots, break the material down even further. In this way, the bacteria and fungi continue the decomposition process begun by insects.

Living things that get their energy from the waste material of others are called decomposers. They swiftly break down fallen leaves and other plant and animal remains. This releases the nutrients locked up in the remains and makes them available for the trees and other plants to use again.

These Australian termites help to break down rain forest plant material.

Unbroken chain

Without the work of the decomposers, the rain forest soil would soon run out of nutrients. Trees, the primary producers of the rain forest, and decomposers, which are the final link in the chain, need each other in order to survive.

Trees provide food for bacteria and fungi in the form of falling leaves. The bacteria and fungi break the leaves down to provide the nutrients that new trees need in order to grow.

Web weaving

Birds and small mammals often eat the larger decomposers, such as ants and millipedes. So the decomposers also find themselves at different points on the food chain. It's all part of the complex rain forest food web.

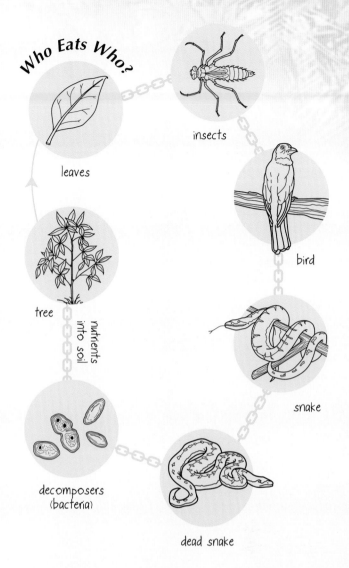

Who Eats Who?

leaves

insects

bird

tree

nutrients into soil

snake

decomposers (bacteria)

dead snake

Fungi, such as these, grow on the rain forest floor.

Treetop chains

If the rain forests are the world's richest habitat, then most of the wealth of wildlife in the forest is found in the treetops. Around nine-tenths of the living things in the rain forest are found in the forest canopy, or overstory.

Canopy cornucopia

The canopy is where the sun shines brightest. Trees, vines, and other plants compete with each other to capture light energy and turn it into useful chemical energy in the form of sugar. Around four-fifths of the food made by rain forest plants is produced high in the treetops.

This insect, called a katydid, lives in the tops of trees.

Fruit treats

All of this plant growth means that there is plenty to eat in the canopy in the form of leaves, shoots, flowers, and fruit. Many rain forest animals spend their entire lives feasting in the treetops and never leave them to go down to the forest floor.

Colorful birds such as parrots, toucans, and hummingbirds fly in the treetops. Climbing animals such as monkeys, frogs, squirrels, and lizards are also found there in large numbers. There are insects everywhere, in a dazzling variety of colors and shapes found nowhere else in the world.

Yummy!

The fisherman bat lives in trees but swoops down over rivers to snatch up fish in its claws.

Fruit bat.

Canopy bats

Bats are so common in rain forests that sometimes there can be more bats there than any other mammal. Many bats eat fruit or take nectar from flowers, which helps to pollinate plants. Other bats eat a lot of insects. A single bat can eat 1,000 mosquitoes in just 1 hour.

Bats are also an important food source for other animals along the food chain. Boa constrictors are very fond of eating bats and will dart out to ambush them. Owls, like bats, are nighttime fliers, and they will also catch bats.

Who Eats Who?

flower

bat

boa

Don't eat me!

Many rain forest insects have incredible camouflage to hide them from the eyes of predators. There are insects that look like twigs, bark, flower parts, dead leaves, living leaves, and even half-eaten leaves.

The leaf-imitating katydid mimics a living green leaf.

Food rewards

Sometimes it seems that plants actually want to be eaten. They produce brightly colored flowers and sweet, fragrant fruits to attract insects and other animals. Of course, there is a good reason for this.

The birds and the bees

Plants, like any other living thing, need to reproduce to make more plants just like themselves. But, being rooted to the spot, a plant can't travel around and find a mate in the way an animal can. So, plants use other creatures to help them out.

For a new plant to grow from a seed, pollen has to be taken from one flower to another in a process known as pollination. When bees and birds visit a flower for sweet, energy-rich pollen and nectar, some of the plant pollen sticks to them and is carried to the next flower they visit.

Yummy!

Strangler fig fruits are eaten by rain forest animals who then leave fig seeds around the treetops in their droppings. When the seeds geminate, they grow a long root all the way down to the forest floor.

South American howler monkeys love eating fruit.

Seed dispersal

Rain forest monkeys, such as spider monkeys, swing effortlessly from branch to branch in the canopy, gathering fruits and nuts. They consume a huge amount of fruit, and many of the seeds they eat pass straight through and out the other end of the monkey unharmed. Safely wrapped in a package of fertilizer in the form of a monkey dropping, the seeds fall to the ground, where they germinate, take root, and grow.

A hummingbird in flight approaches a flower in order to drink the nectar inside.

Yummy!

Hummingbirds' tongues have barbs to hook insects out of flowers.

Hummingbirds and hunters

Hummingbirds are agile fliers and love the sweet nectar produced by rain forest flowers. Often hummingbirds are part of a very short food chain made up of just the bird and its food plant. But certain birds of prey in the rain forest specialize in catching hummingbirds. A hummingbird can find itself in a slightly longer chain that includes a flower, a fruit fly, a hummingbird, and a hawk.

Life in miniature

A large habitat such as the rain forest holds a number of smaller habitats within it. Some are as small as a pool of water trapped by the leaves of a plant. And there are food chains here, too.

At home on the trees

Some rain forest plants are not rooted in the ground but are anchored to tree trunks and branches. But these plants do not feed off the tree. Like other plants, they capture the energy of sunlight in order to survive and grow. All they need is a place to live in the sun!

Many rain forest plants grow high in the trees.

Tree ponds

Bromeliads grow on rain forest trees in South America. They have no roots and take in minerals from rainwater through special hairs in their thick, waterproof leaves, which grow in a circle around the stalk. The rainwater collects in the middle, forming a miniature pond that becomes home to a number of tiny rain forest dwellers.

A bromeliad pond provides insects with water to drink and plant debris on which to feed.

Help from the desert

Bromeliads growing on trees on the east coast of Brazil get their minerals from a remarkable source. They are carried on the wind across the Atlantic Ocean from sandstorms in the Sahara Desert.

Pool chains

More than 250 different types of animals have been found living in bromeliad ponds. The ponds are home to insect larvae, which hatch and grow in the ponds, where they feed on bits of leaf and other plant matter that fall into the pool. In turn, they are eaten by other insect larvae, frogs, and their tadpoles. Fierce dragonfly nymphs sometimes eat the tadpoles.

Decaying leaves and other plant debris in bromeliad pond

insect larvae

tadpole

dragonfly nymph

monkey

This amazingly colored frog lives in bromeliad ponds in the Amazon rain forest.

Up and down the trees

Many animals of the rain forest are expert climbers, so they can spend time at different levels in the forest.

Night foragers

Big-eyed galagos leap fearlessly from branch to branch in the nighttime forests of Africa. Usually they forage high in the treetops, catching insects and eating fruit.

Sometimes, though, a galago might be tempted to come down to the ground in search of a mouse or eggs from a bird's nest. However, a galago isn't quite as agile on the ground as it is in the trees. A sharp-eyed owl can suddenly swoop down and snatch up the galago in its sharp claws.

Galago.

Who Eats Who?

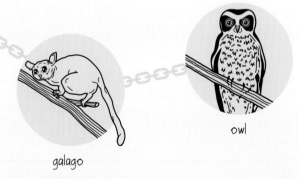

seeds

rodent

galago

owl

Ant farms

Leafcutter ants are unusual among insects because they grow their own food. Parties of leafcutters march out of their underground nests on the forest floor and climb up tree trunks. Using their sharp jaws, they cut up plant leaves and carry the pieces back down the tree to their nest.

Here, they chew the leaves into a pulp, mixing them with saliva. A fungus grows on the chewed-up leaves, which the ants collect and eat. The fungus, not the plant leaves, is the ants' only source of food. So the ants are secondary consumers, not primary consumers as they might at first appear to be.

Ant snacks

Hard-working leafcutter ants don't escape attention in the rain forest. The giant anteater can easily follow the parade of ants back down to their nest. Ripping open the nest with its powerful claws, it scoops up the helpless ants with its long, sticky tongue.

Yummy!

A leafcutter ant can carry a piece of leaf that weighs 50 times more than the ant itself does.

A working party of leafcutter ants.

Life on the ground floor

As mentioned earlier, most rain forest life exists in the treetops. Little light reaches the ground below, so few plants can grow there. This means there is not much food for ground-dwelling animals to eat.

Hunters and collectors

Certain small-sized animals do survive on the rain forest floor by feeding on fruits and seeds that fall from the branches above.

In South American rain forests live cat-sized rodents called agoutis. An agouti has to be alert as it searches for food. Jaguars prowling through the forest will catch and eat agoutis, as will racoon-like coatis.

Agoutis forage for fruit and seeds. Often, they bury seeds to eat later. But sometimes the seeds never get eaten and germinate to grow into new trees.

Adaptable antelopes

Several different kinds of antelopes, called duikers, are found in African rain forests. Each kind has adapted to a particular diet of fruits and nuts. One duiker has a flexible jaw that allows it to eat large pieces of fruit. The main predators of duikers include leopards and pythons.

Agoutis forage on the rain forest floor in South America.

Pig in the wood

Wild pigs, or peccaries, roam the rain forests, rooting around for roots, fruits, insects, and other small animals. With their wide, varied diet, these animals can occupy several different places on the food chain.

Wild pigs are fierce protectors of their territory and don't make easy prey. However, a large hunter, such as a big cat or snake, may still capture an unwary pig by surprise and eat it.

We're in the chain!

The Mbuti people of the Congo region in Africa live in the rain forest. They rely on birds to guide them across the forest floor to wild bees' nests, from which they gather honey to eat.

Wild pigs, or peccaries, eat many kinds of rain forest foods.

Who Eats Who?

fruit

duiker

leopard

Stuck in the middle

Animals in the middle of a food chain have two main food-related concerns. The first is to find enough food to eat. The second is to avoid being eaten.

Slow, slow, quick, quick, slow

Chameleons are a type of lizard found in the forests of Africa, where they hunt for insects in the trees and bushes. A chameleon moves very, very slowly. This has two advantages. First, its insect prey is not aware of its approach, and second, the chameleon avoids attracting the attention of a larger predator.

Once the chameleon gets within striking distance of an insect, it flicks out its long, sticky tongue almost faster than a human eye can follow. The insect has little chance of escaping, and any predator nearby has little chance of spotting the chameleon. After its meal, the chameleon resumes its slow progress.

Yummy!

The three-toed sloth is another animal that relies on moving slowly to escape being seen. The slow sloth can take as long as a month to digest a meal of leaves.

Zap! A chameleon catches its dinner.

24

Colorful confusion

The chameleon has another advantage. It can change colors to blend in to its background. It turns green to match leaves or brown to match bark. Other animals use camouflage, too. The South American emerald boa can't change color, but its bright green coloration makes it hard to spot in the leafy rain forest. So the boa can hunt its prey of birds and other small animals while avoiding being seen by the bigger eagles that would attack and eat it!

Killer spider

In the rain forests of South America, a formidable predator prowls the forest floor. With a legspan of some 10 inches (25 cm), you would not want to find a bird-eating spider in your bath! Bird-eating spiders hunt insects, lizards, and frogs. They will also snatch baby birds from their nests, which is how they get their name. However, bigger animals, such as coatis—a kind of large rodent—will dig into the spider's burrow for an eight-legged snack!

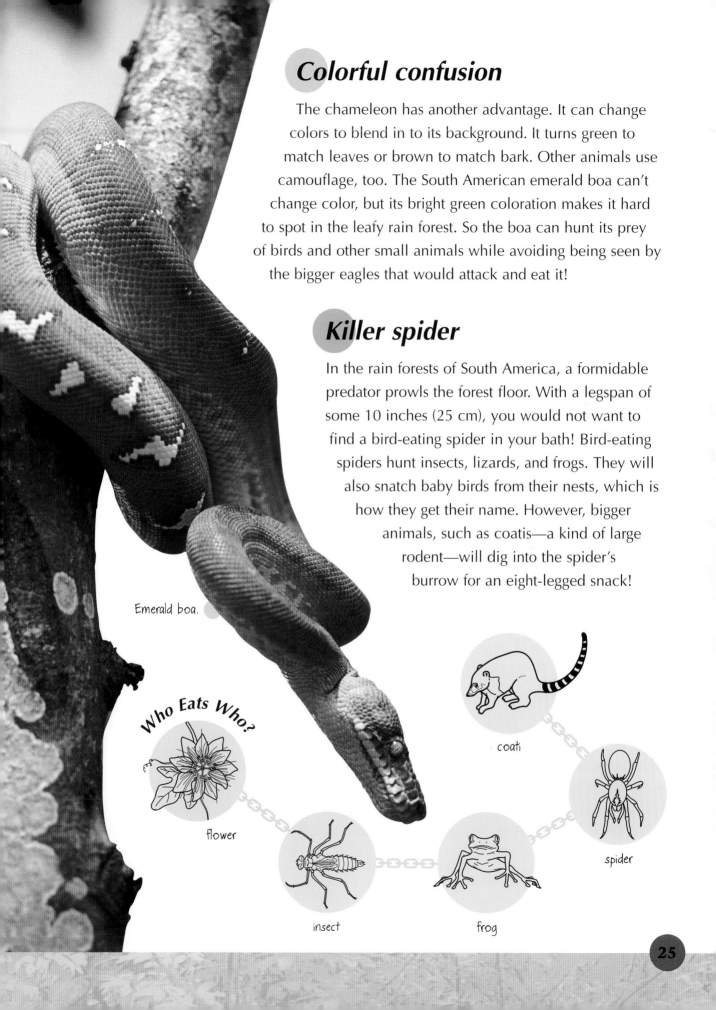

Emerald boa.

Who Eats Who?

flower

insect

frog

coati

spider

Kings of the jungle

At the top of the food chain are the super-predators, the big hunters of the forest. There are never very many large hunters because a lot of energy has been lost this far along the chain, and there isn't much room at the top of the food pyramid. However, these rain forest hunters are among the most skilled predators in the world.

Top cats

Cats are the biggest hunters prowling the rain forest. In Asia, there is the tiger; in South America, the jaguar; and in Africa, the leopard. All of these big cats are formidable hunters. Large animals, such as pigs, are often hard to find in the rain forest, so the cats have adapted to eating smaller ones. The jaguar, for example, is an excellent swimmer and is skilled at catching fish.

The rain forest is also home to smaller cats such as the margay and ocelot of South America and the leopard cat of Asia. These animals are generally not much bigger than a pet cat or small dog. Most of these smaller cats hunt at night. They are agile and lightweight enough to hunt their prey both on the forest floor and up in the canopy.

Aerial attackers

Eagles are big, fearsome predators. The harpy eagles of South America and the monkey-eating eagles of the Philippines are more than three feet (0.9 m) long, with wingspans of up to six and a half feet (2 m).

When an eagle spots its prey, it dives low into the trees and then swoops up again to attack the unsuspecting victim from below. These fast, powerful birds can snatch up small pigs, squirrels, and lemurs. The harpy eagle also preys on slow-moving sloths.

Who Eats Who?

leaves

harpy eagle

sloth

Monkey-eating eagle.

Yummy!

"Jaguar" comes from a Native American word meaning "killer that takes its prey in a single bound."

A black jaguar, also known as a black panther.

Food web

Here is a food web that could be found in a South American rain forest. Surrounding it are some fascinating rain forest facts.

sloth

toucan

leaves
fruit
flowers

frog

insect

Nearly one-third of the total weight of plants in the world grows in rain forests.

The slow-moving sloth is a habitat all by itself. Hundreds of beetles live in its fur, feeding on the algae that grows there.

Some scientists believe that there could be 50 million different kinds of insects living in rain forests.

Up to 350 inches (900 cm) of rain can fall on the rain forest in a year—twice as much as in the wettest parts of the U.S.

The Brazil nut tree produces tough fruits the size of cannon balls. Each fruit contains up to 20 hard-shelled nuts. The trees rely largely on sharp-toothed agoutis for seed dispersal.

owl

The tallest trees in the rain forest can reach a height of 130 feet (40 m).

harpy eagle

bat

jaguar

Each of the world's 900 or so different kinds of fig trees is pollinated only by its own particular kind of fig wasp.

snake

bird

Cecropia trees have special structures under their leaf stems that provide food for fierce Azteca ants. In return, the ants will swiftly attack any other animal that tries to eat the cecropia.

Glossary

adapted
suited to life in a particular environment.

camouflage
markings, shapes, or colors of an animal that make it difficult to see.

canopy
the "roof" of the rain forest; the topmost part of the forest trees.

consumer
an organism that eats another living thing to get energy; primary consumers eat plants; secondary consumers eat animals.

decomposers
living things that feed on and break down dead plants and animals, as well as animal waste.

fertile
able to support growth.

food chain
the feeding links between living things; a guide to who eats whom.

food web
a map of all the feeding links in a habitat showing how plants and animals are connected to each other.

forage
to search for something to eat.

germinate
to start to grow; a seed produces its first root and leaves when it germinates.

habitat
the place where a living thing makes its home.

herbivore
an animal that eats plants.

larva
the young form (the plural is "larvae") of some insects that looks quite different from the adults.

mammal
a warm-blooded animal with fur or hair, such as a leopard or a human. Female mammals produce milk to feed their young.

nutrients
another word for food; nutrients are all the things needed for a balanced diet.

nymph
the young form of some insects, such as dragonflies, that looks similar to the adults.

organism

a living thing.

photosynthesis

the process by which plants capture the energy of sunlight to make sugar.

pollinated

when grains of pollen are carried from one flower to another, usually by bees; when this has happened, seeds can begin to form.

predator

an animal that kills and eats other animals.

prey

animals that are caught and eaten by predators.

producer

an organism that makes, or produces, its own food; producers are the source of energy for the rest of the food chain

recycling

reusing waste materials.

Rain Forest Web Sites

http://www.rainforestheroes.com/kidscorner
Be a hero—help protect the rain forest.

http://www.smm.org/sln/tf/s/strata/strata.html
A simple guide to the layers of the rain forest.

http://www.howstuffworks.com/rainforest.htm
Lots of good, clear information about rain forests and how they work.

http://www.exploratorium.edu/frogs/rainforest/index.html
Sounds of the rain forest to download and listen to!

http://yahooligans.yahoo.com/science_and_nature/the_earth/ecology/rainforests
A directory of rain forest links—ready to click!

Index